I0845052

About the author

Paul Benhaim is one of the world's leading experts on cannabis sativa. He is the author of 9 books and 4 guides, as well as the founder of Cannabis Psychedelics. In the 20th Century, both the UK and in Australia Paul was responsible for the first hemp food companies. Pioneering the first hemp CBD businesses in Australia and Japan as well as building a $500m USA hemp company. Currently Paul is founder and chairman of The Hemp Plastic Company – a business built on producing plastics from this wonder plant.

Paul created the first company in Australia to look at legal production of psilocybin where he designed a clinical trial with a team of world experts.

Paul's first psychedelic experience was at the age of 17, and his journeys with many psychedelics have continued since then, inspiring his passions to work with nature. Having worked with the cannabis plant for three decades it was only recently that Paul recognised the ability for cannabis to be used as a true psychedelic.

An intentional Cannabis Psychedelic experience guided him to work with his global networks to share a well- considered protocol for healing based upon both science and ancient wisdom. This offering is now offered at his home through Cannabis Psychedelics. His direct spiritual connection with the cannabis plant has influenced the offer for legal cannabis users to meet and heal with this plant ally in a sacred, safe and intentional space.

Paul Benhaim

- The history of **Cannabis as a Psychedelic**, and why it has been used for thousands of years

- Cannabis is more than just getting high – it can be used for **deep transformational growth**

- **Mindfulness practice** within the psychedelic landscape

- Specific **meditations** you can practice immediately, and for the rest of your life

- **Trauma healing** through conscious exploration

- What **letting go of the ego** means in science – the default mode network

- Inner exploration beyond LSD – Stanislov Grof's **holotropic breathwork** including some practices for you

- How to navigate the cannabis psychedelic experience with clear **intentions and goal setting**

- Learning the importance of **integration** within the psychedelic experience

- **Awareness of challenges** and how to navigate the complex landscape

- The **legal and ethical considerations** of a cannabis psychedelic experience

- What to do after a cannabis psychedelic experience – **integration circles and community support**

TABLE OF CONTENTS

About The Author 1

Forward 5

Unveiling The Cannabis Psychedelic Experience 7

Cannabis as a vessel of spiritual significance 8
Beyond recreational boundaries 9
Navigating the psychedelic landscape without reference points 9
Embracing the transcendent 10

Mindfulness In The Psychedelic Landscape 12

Cultivating Awareness 15
Synergy Between Mindfulness And Psychedelics 19
Enhancing The Journey 20

Healing Trauma Through Conscious Exploration 23

Gabor Maté's Trauma-Informed Approach 23
Robin Carhart-Harris's Scientific Lens 27
Stanislav Grof's Legacy In Inner Exploration 31

Navigating The Cannabis Psychedelics Mindset 38

Intentions, Mindfulness, And Integration 38
Mindfulness In Action 40
Integration Practices 41

Challenges And Considerations 44

Navigating The Complex Landscape Of Cannabis Psychedelics 44
Navigating Legal And Ethical Terrain 44
Integration As A Lifelong Practice 47
Challenges On The Path 50

Cultivating Mindful Communities 52

The Role Of Connection And Support In The Cannabis Psychedelics
Journey 52
The Power Of Connection 53
Fostering Support Networks 55

Embark On Your Mindful Journey With Cannabis Psychedelics 58

About Cannabis Psychedelics 59

Cannabis was legalised in Australia in 2016. The industry took many years to establish and grow, and 8 years later it seems to have just begun. In 2023 MDMA and psilocybin have been legalised (rescheduled to Schedule 8 by the TGA) as a medicine in Australia. Nearly one year later only one person has gained access.

Cannabis is a traditional psychedelic with a long history and a safety profile that is arguably safer than water.

Using protocols based upon both clinical study design learnt from the latest psychedelic research (psilocybin, DMT, ayahuasca etc.) and ancient techniques used by the Egyptians and Romans blended with modern psychotherapy and psychiatry – a method of using cannabis within a modern techno ritualistic context was born – Cannabis Psychedelics.

In this book, we will focus on some of the foundational qualities that will support a cannabis psychedelic experience – preparation, mindfulness, integration and support. It is our hope you stay open to this brief introduction and know that this is only the start of your journey – we can go deeper when you are ready.

And yes, cannabis is available legally throughout Australia through any approved Doctor and pharmacist, and even more easily available underground. This method of practice is designed to elevate one's experience of cannabis to use it for what it was originally discovered for – a powerful deep and transformational tool.

Plant medicines are not new, but when used with modern techniques we believe these harm minimisation technologies will elevate the user beyond the high.

Let us step into the enchanting realm of altered consciousness. The multifaceted nature of cannabis emerges far beyond its stereotypical association with recreational indulgence – or being a stoner.

Together let us unravel some of the layers of significance intertwined with cannabis psychedelics. It's a journey that transcends the ordinary, beckoning us to venture into the profound dimensions of our consciousness.

Traditionally relegated to the fringes of spiritual and sacred practices, cannabis, with its rich historical tapestry, unveils itself as more than a recreational herb. Its use extends back through time, interwoven with rituals and ceremonies that tapped into its potential as a conduit to realms beyond the mundane. With historical records dating back thousands of years, from ancient China, Rome and India – it is with particular interest we find the use of an early form of cannabis vaporisation used for psychedelic and spiritual use over 2000 years ago.

Beyond recreational boundaries

Contrary to its common portrayal as a mere recreational substance, cannabis reveals itself as a sacred ally in the exploration of altered states. With Australia legalising Cannabis in 2016, it is finally time to begin to dismantle preconceptions, recognizing the potential for cannabis to serve as a profound catalyst for self-discovery and inner growth.

Navigating the psychedelic landscape without reference points

Unlike other psychedelics that may necessitate external guidance, cannabis possesses a unique quality. It empowers seekers to embark on journeys without the constraints of predetermined maps. The art of a cannabis psychedelic experience is in the 'simple' art of allowing cannabis to guide us through the uncharted territories of our minds.

Invoking intention in exploration

Though the cannabis psychedelic experience is not a passive endeavour; it invites us to set intentions, establishing a purposeful engagement with the plant's transformative potential. There exists a nuanced dance between intentionality and surrender, understanding that the cannabis experience is both personal and collective. And it is the collective evolution that inspires us to offer group cannabis psychedelic experiences today.

Embracing the transcendent

Within the folds of cannabis's psychoactive embrace, seekers often report encounters with the transcendent—a sense of interconnectedness with the cosmos. Having a mystical experience is great. Though we explore these experiences, recognizing the potential for cannabis to be a key to unlocking profound insights into the nature of self and existence AND incorporating these experiences into the users' lives forever onwards.

The rich tapestry of cannabis psychedelic experiences paves the way for deeper exploration. Together, in the next chapters let us, together delve into the harmonious integration of mindfulness in the psychedelic landscape, adding layers of depth to our understanding of this unique and transformative journey. Join us as we continue to unveil the mysteries that lie within the union of cannabis psychedelics and mindfulness.

A practical guide to transformative meditations

As we embark on the expansive landscapes of the mind, mindfulness emerges as a beacon, guiding seekers through the intricate tapestry of altered consciousness. It is our goal to bring this weaving into your daily life, so let us delve into the practical dimensions of mindfulness, where you will be offered detailed instructions for transformative meditations that harmonize with the psychedelic experience. By grounding ourselves in the present moment, we cultivate a profound connection with our inner selves, laying the groundwork for a transformative exploration.

- When do we recommend you begin mindfulness? Now.

- How often should you practice? As often as possible, until it is a way of life.

- Where is this helpful? In every aspect of your life – whether as a student, a teacher, a lover or a mother.

The power of presence

At the heart of the psychedelic journey lies the transformative potential of mindfulness. So let us begin with the mindfulness part today.

1. To cultivate a deep sense of presence, find a quiet space where you won't be disturbed.

2. Sit comfortably*, close your eyes*, and turn your attention inward.

3. Begin by focusing on your breath, allowing it to flow naturally.

4. Gradually, bring your awareness to the sensations in your body, acknowledging any tension or discomfort.

5. With each breath, release any tension, surrendering to the present moment.

6. Expand your awareness to include sounds, sensations, and thoughts, allowing them to come and go without attachment.

7. Repeat.

This seemingly simple practice enhances your ability to navigate the ebbs and flows of life, as well as within the psychedelic experiences with grace and inner stability. This is powerful.

- Sitting comfortably. How to do this depends on your personal needs. Find a seat or lay down – whatever keeps your back straight, without you falling asleep. Often sitting on high cushions with your feet on the floor is found to be helpful

Cultivating awareness

Practical mindfulness meditations become tools for heightened self-awareness within the psychedelic landscape. Let's try one of my favourites.

Meta bhavna (Loving-Kindness)

1. Find a comfortable seated position and close your eyes.

2. Begin by directing loving-kindness toward yourself. Silently repeat phrases like "May I be happy, may I be healthy, may I be free from the chains that bind me."

3. Expand this loving-kindness to others, starting with loved ones, then acquaintances, and finally extending it universally to all beings.

4. Repeat.

5. Allow the feelings of love and compassion to permeate your being, creating a nurturing space within.

Breath focus

1. Sit comfortably with your spine straight and shoulders relaxed.

2. Close your eyes and bring your attention to your breath.

3. Focus on the natural rhythm of your breath, observing the inhalation and exhalation. Focus on the place where the breath enters and exits your body.

4. If your mind wanders, gently redirect your attention to the breath without judgment.

This practice cultivates centred awareness, grounding you in the present moment.

Walking meditation

1. Choose a quiet space for walking, indoors or outdoors.

2. Walk at a slower pace than usual, maintaining awareness of each step. No, slower.

3. Pay attention to the sensations in your feet as they lift and touch the ground.

4. Coordinate your breath with your steps, creating a rhythmic flow.

5. Engage all your senses, observing the sights, sounds, and smells around you.

This meditation fosters mindfulness in motion, allowing you to explore the interconnected dance between movement and breath.

The above has been my meditations since I first discovered a Vipassana temple on Koh Phagn Ngan in 1992.

Synergy between mindfulness and psychedelics

The interplay between mindfulness and psychedelic experiences is deliberate, forming a dance of consciousness. Integrate mindfulness into your psychedelic journey by consciously directing your attention. Use breath awareness to navigate the inner terrain with purpose and intention, allowing the breath to guide you through the peaks and valleys of the experience.

Having the practice of the above exercises (or even just one) is something to fall back upon when the default mode network is paused in a psychedelic experience and your ego has little, if anything to hold onto.

Mindfulness becomes a potent ally, enhancing the depth of the psychedelic experience. Consciously direct your attention to specific aspects of the journey, such as visuals, emotions, pain or pleasure, or insights. This intentional focus allows for a more profound connection with the psychedelic encounter, transcending the boundaries of ordinary perception.

Integration beyond the experience

Mindfulness extends beyond the psychedelic journey itself; it becomes a lifelong practice. Here we lay the foundation for the integration of mindfulness into daily life, offering tools and insights for weaving the lessons learned during psychedelic exploration into the fabric of everyday existence.

As we immerse ourselves in the interplay between mindfulness and cannabis psychedelics, we pave the way for a richer understanding of their transformative potential. As we unravel the intricacies of this union, embracing the profound journey toward inner growth join us as we continue to explore the synergies between cannabis psychedelics and mindfulness, uncovering the tapestry of wisdom woven within.

Journal, journal, journal. Having a pen and paper (preferably over an electronic device) where you have previously scrawled your goals and intentions ready for immediately after your cannabis psychedelic experience is crucial. Here is where the integration and ongoing life changes are made. Write. Anything. Start with a word, a feeling, your experience, memories and whatever comes. Take your time. Breathe. Meditate. Write some more. Check in again with your prose, later in the day, the week, the month, and before your next journey. This is a record of where you have come from, and which direction you are headed with your inner work.

A holistic approach with Cannabis Psychedelics and mindfulness

In the journey of self-discovery, there follows an intricate terrain of healing trauma through the harmonious blend of cannabis psychedelics and mindfulness. Guided by the trauma-informed approach of Gabor Maté, we explore practical techniques and insights that empower individuals to embark on a transformative path towards emotional and psychological well-being.

Gabor Maté's trauma-informed approach

Gabor Maté's insights serve as a compass, directing us towards a conscious exploration of trauma using cannabis psychedelics and mindfulness.

Mindful self-compassion meditation

1. Find a quiet and comfortable space, either seated or lying down.

2. Close your eyes and focus on your breath, allowing it to bring you into the present moment.

3. As you breathe in, acknowledge any pain or discomfort associated with past traumas.

4. On the exhale, offer yourself words of compassion, such as "May I be free from suffering, may I find peace."

5. Extend this compassion outward, recognizing the shared human experience of suffering.

Cannabis-assisted inner child work

1. Create a safe and nurturing environment for self-reflection.

2. Consume a moderate dose of cannabis, allowing its subtle alterations to open the door to your subconscious.

3. Visualize encountering your inner child—a representation of your vulnerable, wounded self.

4. Engage in a compassionate dialogue, offering comfort, support, and understanding to your past self.

5. Ask your inner child how it feels. Listen.

6. Ask your inner child what it needs to heal. Listen.

7. Ask your inner child if there is anything left. Follow.

8. Allow the combination of cannabis and mindfulness to facilitate a profound and healing reconnection with your inner child.

Cannabis and body-centred mindfulness

1. Begin with a moderate dose of cannabis, focusing on its impact on heightened bodily awareness.

2. Engage in body-scan mindfulness meditation, directing your attention to each part of your body sequentially. Slowly.

3. Notice any sensations, tensions, or emotions without judgment, allowing the cannabis to deepen your connection with your physical self.

4. You may choose to stretch and relax each body part as you move along. Take your time.

5. Through this integrated practice, foster a sense of unity between mind and body, promoting a holistic approach to healing trauma.

Mindful reflection and integration

Remember, whatever experience you choose

1. After the cannabis experience, set aside time for mindful reflection.

2. Journal your thoughts, feelings, and insights gained during the cannabis-assisted exploration.

3. Integrate these reflections into your daily mindfulness practice, allowing the lessons learned to become a part of your ongoing healing journey.

As we navigate the intricate path of healing trauma through the synergy of cannabis psychedelics and mindfulness, this chapter invites individuals to engage in practices that foster compassion, self-awareness, and holistic well-being. The transformative potential of this holistic approach unfolds, offering a roadmap for those seeking profound healing and growth.

Navigating the neurological landscape of Cannabis Psychedelics

Let's move to a slightly more scientific exploration guided by the insights of Robin Carhart-Harris, a leading neuroscientist in the field of psychedelics. By delving into the neurological landscape of cannabis psychedelics, we seek to understand the profound changes occurring within the brain and the transformative potential of altered states of consciousness.

Mapping the psychedelic brain

Robin Carhart-Harris's research has shed light on the intricate dance between cannabis psychedelics and the brain's neural networks. This section offers a closer look at the neural mechanisms at play during psychedelic experiences.

Default Mode Network (DMN) and ego dissolution

1. Carhart-Harris's studies highlight the suppression of the Default Mode Network (DMN) during psychedelic experiences.

2. This suppression leads to a dissolution of the ego, allowing individuals to transcend their habitual thought patterns and perceive reality from a novel perspective.

Understanding the interplay between the DMN and ego dissolution provides insights into the potential for profound self-discovery and personal transformation. It is without these limitations (which are helpful in daily life) that we have the opportunity to build new pathways. It is still us that needs to do the work. The plants are simply a tool to take off the breaks from this ability.

Carhart-Harris's research also suggests increased connectivity between brain regions during psychedelic states. This heightened connectivity may contribute to the synesthetic experiences reported by individuals, where sensory perceptions intermingle. Exploring the enhanced connectivity offers a glimpse into the potential for expanded consciousness and a deeper connection with the fabric of reality.

The intersection of science and spirituality

Carhart-Harris emphasizes the convergence of scientific understanding and spiritual dimensions within psychedelic experiences.

Spiritual epiphanies and neural reorganization

Scientific studies indicate that psychedelic experiences often lead to profound spiritual insights and a sense of interconnectedness. Carhart-Harris proposes that these experiences may be linked to the reorganization of neural pathways, allowing for a broader perspective on self and existence. Bridging the gap between science and spirituality, we unravel the potential for cannabis psychedelics to catalyze transcendent experiences. Not just for you, but for the community we call humanity. Imagine what a difference this could make if everyone had the opportunity to try this.

Therapeutic potential and neural plasticity

Carhart-Harris's work underscores the therapeutic potential of psychedelics, including cannabis, in treating mental health conditions. The concept of neural plasticity, the brain's ability to reorganize and form new connections, aligns with the idea that psychedelic experiences can break ingrained thought patterns. We explore the implications of this neuroplasticity on mental health and well-being, envisioning a future where cannabis psychedelics play a role in therapeutic interventions.

Cannabis psychedelics may offer the opportunity to shed light on the neurological transformations occurring within the brain. Together we weave the threads of science, spirituality, and mindfulness in the pursuit of inner growth and understanding.

Nurturing the psychedelic journey

This chapter takes us deep into the legacy of Stanislav Grof, a pioneering researcher in LSD therapy, providing insights that resonate within the context of cannabis psychedelics and mindfulness.

Guided by Grof's holistic approach, we explore the transformative potential of cannabis psychedelics as a tool for accelerated personal growth and inner exploration.

Beyond LSD therapy

Stanislav Grof's expansive body of work extends beyond the realm of LSD therapy, encompassing a broader vision of inner exploration. This section examines the core principles that define Grof's legacy and their relevance to the use of cannabis psychedelics.

Holotropic breathwork and altered states

Grof's Holotropic Breathwork is a technique that induces altered states of consciousness through controlled breathing. The parallels between Holotropic Breathwork and cannabis psychedelics are profound, considering the potential for both to unlock transformative experiences and access deep layers of the psyche.

Understanding the role of breath in navigating altered states adds a practical dimension to the exploration of cannabis psychedelics.

Grof's emphasis on the interconnectedness of mind, spirit, and personal growth aligns with the holistic potential of cannabis psychedelics. The concept of transcending personal boundaries leads us to explore how cannabis can act as a catalyst for expanded consciousness and a deeper connection with the universal fabric of existence.

The integration of Grof's teachings enhances our understanding of the profound possibilities that cannabis psychedelics offer for self-discovery and spiritual exploration.

Integration into therapeutic practice

Stanislav Grof's work has laid the groundwork for integrating psychedelic experiences into therapeutic settings. Let us look at the practical implications of incorporating cannabis psychedelics into therapeutic practices, guided by Grof's pioneering insights.

Archetypal and perinatal dimensions

Grof's exploration of archetypal dimensions and perinatal experiences provides a framework for understanding the symbolic and transformative nature of psychedelic journeys. Cannabis psychedelics can evoke archetypal themes and facilitate a revisiting of birth experiences, potentially contributing to profound healing and personal growth.

Mindful integration sessions

As we have shared in previous chapters, Grof also emphasises integrating psychedelic experiences into daily life. Mindfulness practices as found in previous chapters can enhance the integration process, allowing individuals to embody the lessons learned during cannabis psychedelic journeys.

Let us now look at 3 examples of holotropic breathwork exercises based upon Grof's work:

Holotropic Breathwork, developed by Stanislav Grof, is a method of self-exploration and therapy that combines deep, rhythmic breathing with evocative music to access non-ordinary states of consciousness. When combined with a psychedelic journey, it can enhance the overall experience. However, it's crucial to approach such practices with caution, responsibility, and respect for the potential risks associated with psychedelic use. Always ensure a safe and supportive environment, preferably with experienced and certified Cannabis Psychedelic Facilitators.

1. Preparation and grounding exercise: "Rooting Breath"

Before diving into the psychedelic journey, it's essential to establish a sense of grounding and security. This exercise focuses on connecting with the earth and establishing a stable foundation:

- **Instructions:**

    - Begin with a few minutes of relaxed breathing to centre yourself.

    - Imagine roots extending from the base of your spine into the earth.

    - Inhale deeply, visualizing energy flowing up through these roots into your body.

    - Exhale slowly, allowing any tension or negativity to be released back into the earth.

- Sync your breath with the sensation of being anchored and supported by the earth.

- **Music:**

  - Choose grounding and rhythmic music with a steady beat to enhance the connection with the earth.

2. **Exploration and release exercise: "Surrendering Breath"**

Once grounded, move into a more exploratory phase to facilitate the release of emotions and unconscious material:

- **Instructions:**

  - Increase the intensity of your breath, moving into a faster and more rhythmic pattern.

  - Allow your breath to become a continuous cycle with minimal pauses between inhalation and exhalation.

  - Focus on surrendering to the breath, letting go of any resistance or control.

  - Encourage the exploration of emotions, memories, or sensations that arise.

- **Music:**

  - Choose evocative and diverse music that supports a range of emotional experiences, from intense to serene, guiding the journey through various emotional landscapes.

3. Integration and healing exercise: "Heart-Centered Breath"

As the psychedelic journey begins to wind down, transition into a heart-centred breathwork exercise to promote integration and healing:

- **Instructions:**

    - Shift the focus of your breath towards the heart centre.

    - Inhale deeply into the chest area, expanding the heart space.

    - Exhale slowly, releasing any residual tension or emotions stored in the heart.

    - Cultivate feelings of compassion, love, and acceptance toward yourself and others.

- **Music:**

    - Choose calming and uplifting music with soothing melodies to support the integration process.

Remember that the combination of holotropic breathwork and psychedelics can be intense, potentially leading to powerful and challenging experiences. It's crucial to approach these practices with a responsible mindset and, ideally, under the guidance of experienced Cannabis Psychedelic Facilitators who understand both modalities. Additionally, always prioritize safety, set, and setting to create a supportive environment for the journey in.

Intentions, mindfulness, and integration

We shift our focus towards practical guidance on navigating the cannabis psychedelic mindset. Drawing on the collective wisdom of visionaries, we explore the importance of setting intentions, approaching the experience with mindfulness, and integrating the insights gained into everyday life.

Setting intentions

Approaching a cannabis psychedelic experience with intentionality is akin to charting a course for exploration. Would you leave home without knowing where you are going? Maybe, but if you want to get somewhere specific, is this the best option?

Let us delve into the significance of setting clear intentions and how they shape the trajectory of the psychedelic journey.

Reflective contemplation

1. Begin by engaging in reflective contemplation before the experience. Use meditations as found earlier in this book.

2. Consider your motivations, desires, and what you hope to gain from the journey.

3. Craft specific and positive intentions, guiding the experience towards personal growth, insight, or healing.

4. This process enhances mindfulness by bringing conscious awareness to the purpose of the cannabis psychedelic exploration.

Sacred rituals and mindful beginnings

1. Treat the consumption of cannabis psychedelics as a sacred ritual.

2. Create a dedicated space and time for the experience, fostering a mindful beginning.

3. Incorporate rituals that hold personal significance, such as lighting candles, expressing gratitude, or engaging in a moment of silence.

4. Cultivating a mindful entry into the experience establishes a foundation for intentional exploration.

Mindfulness in action

Hopefully by now you get the importance of the role of mindfulness during the cannabis psychedelic experience, emphasizing its ability to enhance the depth and quality of the journey.

Breath awareness and flow

1. Focus on breath awareness throughout the experience.

2. Use conscious breathing to anchor yourself in the present moment, especially during moments of heightened intensity.

3. Embrace the ebb and flow of the experience, allowing mindfulness to guide you through the various states of consciousness.

Observation without attachment

1. Cultivate a state of detached observation.

2. Notice thoughts, emotions, and sensations without becoming overly identified with them.

3. This mindful observation fosters a sense of inner distance, allowing for a more objective exploration of the psyche.

Integration practices

The psychedelic journey extends beyond the experience itself; integration is a crucial phase for weaving insights into the fabric of everyday life.

Journaling and creative expression

We have already discussed the importance of dedicating time to post-experience journaling. Document thoughts, feelings, and insights gained during the journey. Explore creative expressions such as art, music, or poetry as a means of processing and integrating the experience.

Mindful application in daily life

Now, extend mindfulness into daily practices. Apply the lessons learned during the cannabis psychedelic journey to navigate challenges, foster personal growth, and cultivate a more mindful and intentional life.

As we navigate the cannabis psychedelic mindset with intention and mindfulness our cannabis psychedelic experience may offer us a guide for individuals seeking a purposeful and transformative exploration. The multifaceted dimensions of cannabis psychedelics allow us to blend practical insights with the wisdom of visionaries and the principles of mindfulness to be the change we want to be in our lives.

Navigating the complex landscape of Cannabis Psychedelics

Like in every work, the complex terrain brings on potential challenges and considerations which are also inherent in the use of cannabis psychedelics. From legal and ethical considerations to the ongoing process of integration, we navigate the multifaceted landscape with mindfulness and intentional awareness.

Navigating legal and ethical terrain

The legal and ethical dimensions surrounding the use of cannabis psychedelics are intricate and ever-evolving. This section guides approaching these considerations with awareness and responsibility.

Legal status and current landscape

1. Understand the current legal status of cannabis psychedelics in your jurisdiction.

2. Stay informed about any changes in regulations, recognizing the dynamic nature of legal landscapes.

3. Approach cannabis psychedelic use with a consciousness of legal implications, advocating for responsible and informed choices.

In Australia, cannabis is Federally (and therefore in every state) legal for medicinal use. In the ACT it is also permissible to grow for your use, your own medicine. That is wonderful if you live in the ACT.

For most people though, you will need to get a prescription from your Doctor (search Google for 'Cannabis Doctor near me' or similar), who will then prescribe you (presuming you meet the current criteria).

If you want more details then you may find more information from the TGA and the Australian Prescribers guide to medicinal cannabis.

After you have a prescription, you can then have this fulfilled by a pharmacist (via a chemist or dispensary) online and have it sent to your door! You may also take it to your local chemist and they can fulfil it (if they don't have it in stock, they order it in – so best to call first).

Consuming cannabis via vape or smoke has the same legalities as tobacco smoking.

Edibles you can consume anywhere.

You can also fly with your cannabis, as long as the place you are flying to has federally legal cannabis (such as within Australia, Thailand etc).

Note: it is NOT legal to drive with cannabis in your system, even if you are not intoxicated. This makes little sense, as you can have opiates and alcohol in your system if not inebriated. This is likely to change, but until it does be aware.

Please check the latest laws, as laws around cannabis are changing rapidly.

Ethical considerations

1. Reflect on the ethical dimensions of personal and communal psychedelic use.

2. Consider the potential impact on others and the environment, fostering a mindful approach to ethical decision-making.

3. Engage in open dialogue and share insights within the psychedelic community to collectively navigate ethical challenges. Integration circles and groups like Cannabis Psychedelics are good places to start. Or start your own.

Integration as a lifelong practice

Integration is not merely a post-experience reflection but a lifelong practice. Let us explore the ongoing process of weaving the lessons learned during cannabis psychedelic experiences into the fabric of daily life. Repeating these lessons we hope you will not just 'get it' but live this reality.

Mindful reflection and continuous learning

1. Schedule regular periods of mindful reflection, allowing the integration process to unfold over time.

2. Embrace a stance of continuous learning, remaining open to new insights and perspectives.

3. Cultivate a growth-oriented mindset, recognizing that personal evolution is an ongoing and iterative process.

Community support and connection

1. Seek community support through psychedelic integration groups or trusted individuals. If one doesn't exist, consider starting your own.

2. Share experiences, challenges, and insights within a supportive and understanding community.

3. Establish meaningful connections with like-minded individuals, fostering a sense of belonging and shared wisdom.

Challenges on the path

Cannabis psychedelics, like any transformative tool, may present challenges. This section explores potential difficulties and how mindfulness can be applied to navigate them.

Integration difficulties

1. Acknowledging challenges in integrating psychedelic experiences is an important first step.

2. Use mindfulness to explore resistance, emotional blocks, or conflicting insights that may arise.

3. Consider seeking professional support or guidance to navigate integration difficulties with mindfulness and self-compassion. There are now many trauma-informed, cannabis psychedelic psychotherapists and psychiatrists available to support your journey. Cannabis Psychedelics can recommend you someone in your area who maybe able to support you via online sessions if you contact us.

Cultural and societal paradigms

1. Reflect on the cultural and societal paradigms that may influence your relationship with cannabis psychedelics. Your past beliefs about cannabis, your past experiences. Your family and community beliefs.

2. Approach these influences with awareness, questioning societal norms and cultivating a mindful autonomy in your choices.

3. Advocate for a nuanced and informed discourse surrounding cannabis psychedelics within larger societal conversations. Bring up these subjects on social media and be proud you are on the cutting edge of mental health technologies.

So once you have considered the legal and ethical foundations, integrated mindfulness techniques, and have an awareness of how to deal with challenges – the chances are high that you will have a wonderful experience with cannabis psychedelics.

Cultivating mindful communities

This chapter explores the significance of mindful communities in the context of cannabis psychedelics. Building connections, fostering support networks, and engaging in open dialogue create a shared space for growth, learning, and the responsible exploration of altered states of consciousness.

The power of connection

Connection with others on similar journeys can profoundly impact the cannabis psychedelic experience. This section delves into the transformative potential of building mindful connections within the psychedelic community.

Community as a catalyst for growth

Recognize the potential for shared experiences within a community setting – consider a group experience (especially if you have had an initial one on one). Engage in open and honest communication, creating a space for individuals to share insights, challenges, and transformative moments. Embrace the diversity of perspectives within the community, fostering an environment of mutual respect and understanding.

Tap into the collective wisdom of the community. Learn from the experiences of others, gaining insights that may enhance your journey. Participate in group discussions, workshops, or online forums to expand your understanding of cannabis psychedelics through shared learning.

Cannabis Psychedelics has a Facebook group for this and a private group for people who have had a cannabis psychedelic experience already.

https://www.facebook.com/THCpsychedelics

We recommend that those wanting to get a deeper understanding of the work consider the Cannabis Psychedelic Facilitator Training Course. You don't have to take it up as a profession, teach or support others on this journey (though you will be capable of doing this after the course). It may simply be what you need to have the strong foundation to move forward in life learning the wisdom of the experts in this field.

Support networks play a crucial role in navigating the complexities of the cannabis psychedelic experience. Supportive connections contribute to individual growth and well-being.

Peer support and integration circles

Seek or create peer support groups or integration circles focused on cannabis psychedelics. These are places where you may share your experiences within a safe and supportive space, receiving insights and feedback from others.

Find a close friend or confidante to establish your network of trusted individuals who can offer guidance and encouragement throughout your journey. We at Cannabis Psychedelics will be your friend if you need ☺

Professional guidance and therapeutic support

Consider seeking professional guidance from therapists or counsellors experienced in psychedelic integration. Many have experienced Cannabis Psychedelics now and are fully qualified psychotherapists and psychologists who are available to support you – just contact us mailto:connect@cannabispsychedelics.com.au to find out more. Professional support provides a structured and confidential space for exploring the challenges and insights that may arise during cannabis psychedelic experiences. Balance community support with the expertise of professionals, creating a holistic approach to your psychedelic journey.

Open and mindful dialogue is essential for the growth and sustainability of psychedelic communities. We support fostering respectful conversations that contribute to the collective wisdom of the community.

Promoting inclusivity and diversity

Create inclusive spaces that welcome diverse perspectives and backgrounds. Recognize and address biases or prejudices within the community, fostering an environment where everyone feels respected and valued. Embrace the richness that comes from a diverse and inclusive community. These offerings allow the consideration of others perspectives *without judgement*. This in itself is a form of mindfulness that the author has found valuable in his life.

Responsible communication about Cannabis Psychedelics

Engage in responsible and informed communication about cannabis psychedelics. Don't make stuff up you are not sure is backed by fact.

Share experiences with mindfulness, avoiding sensationalism or misinformation. There is no need to exaggerate your experiences. Often it is hard to put into words experiences that are otherworldly, where you connect with everything. Using feeling words, paintings, dance and other expressions can be just as important a form of communication. Words are not always helpful.

Whatever you choose to contribute we know that together we can shape a positive and accurate narrative surrounding the responsible use of cannabis psychedelics within the broader community and, who knows, maybe the world will change for the better.

Thanks for joining us on what we hope has been an insightful exploration into the realm of cannabis psychedelics. We invite you to continue your journey towards inner growth and self-discovery. The wisdom shared in these chapters, blending the profound insights of visionaries, practical guidance, and the principles of mindfulness, forms a tapestry that can enrich your experiences with cannabis psychedelics.

And the journey has just begun, together. So let us create the best experience we can, and be mindful of ongoing improvement and supporting each other in this journey through good communication, empathy and appreciation for each other.

Thank you.

About cannabis psychedelics

We are focused on supporting the healing of others through intentional and safe settings for deep transformational experiences through the use of cannabis sativa.

To further enhance your understanding and connect with a community of like-minded individuals, we invite you to visit our dedicated platform: www.cannabispsychedelics.com.au. Here, you'll find a wealth of resources, community forums, and expert insights to support you on your journey.

Our Facebook page is https://www.facebook.com/THCpsychedelics- please like and share.

Our platform is designed to foster mindful connections, provide up-to-date information, and create a space for open dialogue about the responsible use of cannabis psychedelics. Join our community of seekers, explorers, and visionaries as we continue to share knowledge, experiences, and collective wisdom.

Enjoy our FAQ   – full of lots of information about our experiences.
https://cannabispsychedelics.com.au/faq/
Enjoy learning about our Programs – learn about our private, group and online opportunities, as well as our weeklong immersion in Thailand, or the Nine Perfect Strangers retreat!
https://cannabispsychedelics.com.au/programs/

Facilitator Training – maybe this is for you? Just email us for a course curriculum: connect@cannabispsychedelics.com.au .

Remember, the journey with cannabis psychedelics is a unique and personal adventure. With mindfulness as your guide, you have the opportunity to unlock profound insights, nurture personal growth, and contribute to a community that values shared learning.

Embark on this transformative path with intentionality, and may your exploration of cannabis psychedelics be filled with mindfulness, connection, and a deeper understanding of the inner landscapes that await you.

Oh, and if you haven't yet entered – do make sure you have registered to win a free VIP experience for you or a loved one – all you need to do is share the email of the person you want to win here:

https://cannabispsychedelics.com.au/competition/

Paul and the team at Cannabis Psychedelics.